THE
NEW
TESTAMENT
in
Limerick Verse

THE
NEW
TESTAMENT
in
Limerick Verse

CHRISTOPHER

GOODWINS

John Hunt
Publishing Limited

Copyright © 2001 John Hunt Publishing Ltd
Text © 2001 Christopher Goodwins

ISBN 1 84298 031 9

Designed by Jim Weaver Design

All rights reserved. Except for brief quotations in critical
articles or reviews, no part of this book may be
reproduced in any manner without prior written
permission from the publishers.

Write to:
John Hunt Publishing Ltd
46A West Street
Alresford
Hampshire SO24 9AU
UK

The rights of Christopher Goodwins as author of this
work have been asserted in accordance with the
Copyright, Designs and Patents Act 1988.

A CIP catalogue record for this book is available
from the British Library.

Printed in Guernsey, Channel Islands

CONTENTS

ABOUT THIS BOOK

I don't think that anybody has put the New Testament into limerick format before! Maybe *The New Testament in Limerick Verse* is unique! Anyhow, the object of the exercise is to encourage you to read your Bibles after reading this. If you are new to the New Testament, then this will give you an insight into what it's about – and I hope that it will be very easy for you to read, remember, and learn.

CHRISTOPHER GOODWINS
Priest-in-Charge of St. Andrew's,
Isleham, Cambridgeshire
July 2001

ABOUT THE AUTHOR

After thirty-seven years in the Church, Christopher Goodwins retired in 1998. In addition to his church activities, his career has included work as a broadcaster; choral scholar at St. John's College, Cambridge; keen traveller and, of late, a qualified pilot.

Christopher's public interests include working with young people and with senior citizens and, amongst his many pursuits, has recently added a new string to his bow – writing.

The following verses explain how he came to write the limericks in this book.

An Isleham Vicar called Chris
Wrote Scripture in limericks. *"This*
Should help people read,
About Jesus, indeed,
And enjoy it, – not give Him a miss!"

So he put pen to paper in Lent,
And through the New Testament went.
It seemed rather fun
When he realised he'd done
Something no one had thought to invent!

In three weeks, his verse went world-wide,
On radio, TV, – inside
Every paper on sale!
"It's for female and male –
Just read about Jesus!" – he cried.

I hope you will read the real thing –
Inspired by these verses, and sing
God's praises each day
As you go on your way!
One day, I'll *record* them! – like *Bing!*

MATTHEW 1

In Matthew, the family tree
Shows Jesus was born Royalty!
Searched each generation
Of the Jewish nation –
From Abraham to 6BC.

MATTHEW 2: 1–2

Wise men from the east came to see
Where the King of the Jews was born. 'We
Saw his star in the sky
And we're just passing by,
To worship Him. Where can He be?'

MATTHEW 2: 1–8

In Bethlehem, Judah, a son
For Joseph and Mary – the One
Was born King of the Jews.
Then King Herod got news.
'Find this child!' Herod stormed. 'No King! None!'

MATTHEW 2: 9–10

They followed the star all the way
To Bethlehem, where the child lay
In a stable that night.
When they saw him, the sight
Was one of exceeding great joy!

MATTHEW 2: 11

So they offered their gifts then and there:
Gold, frankincense, myrrh they prepare
For the King of the Jews.
Tinged with sadness, the news –
Of the suffering the Christ child should bear!

MATTHEW 2: 12

The wise men used wisdom that night
And avoided King Herod like blight!
They travelled a way
Which was safer, so they
Returned home, after seeing *The Light!*

MATTHEW 2: 13

King Herod was not very pleased
To be given the slip. His diseased
Old body was racked
With revenge. 'I want hacked
To death, all infants!' he wheezed.

MATTHEW 2: 13–14

But Joseph was warned in a dream
To escape into Egypt. 'This team
Has saved our child's life!'
Joseph said to his wife.
Two years' safety, at last, it would seem.

MATTHEW 2: 19–23

News now came that Herod was dead.
'It's safe to go back!' Joseph said.
To Galilee truly
They travelled, and duly
Made a home there, to Nazareth led.

MATTHEW 3: 1–16

Baptising in Jordan, John came –
'Repent, for the Kingdom!' – his claim.
'Not worthy – no, never!'
Dipped Jesus in river.
His cousin was never the same!

MATTHEW 3: 16–17

The moment of truth came about
When John lifted Jesus right out
Of the water. 'My Son' –
Said a voice – 'is the one
In whom I am pleased! Without doubt!'

MATTHEW 4: 1–9

The time came for Jesus to think
Of his future. The devil would wink
If he turned stones to bread
Ruled the world, or be led
To jump over the temple's high brink.

MATTHEW 4: 10–11

The scriptures are so very clear
'Don't tempt God!' it says, 'So I fear
Your efforts are wasted!
Now Satan – you're pasted!
Don't ever come tempting me here!'

MATTHEW 4: 12–13

At this stage, the Lord moved his base
From Nazareth to seaside place.
'Capernaum's home
For me now! Let us roam
Throughout Galilee, preaching apace!'

MATTHEW 4: 18–25

He gathered a small group of men
Who would learn from him everything, then
Be his right-hand people
From temple to steeple
And spread the Good News. 'Master, when?'

MATTHEW 5–7

'Just wait till I've taught you, my friends'
Said Jesus, 'and my Spirit sends
You power from on high
Makes you bolder, and I
Will be Shepherd. And that's how God tends!'

MATTHEW 5: 2–12

He taught the crowds on a hill
About blessings, and what is God's will.
'Be good to each other,
And do love your brother!
Be kind and be helpful. Don't kill!'

MATTHEW 5: 3–12

Jesus taught 'The poor would be blessed,
The bereaved, the meek, and the rest,
Those who hunger and thirst
And make peace, will be first
In the Kingdom of God. They'll be best!'

MATTHEW 5: 13–16

'It's no good concealing a light
It's got to be useful at night!
Just be like the salt
That brings flavour out. Halt
Whatever is evil. All right?'

MATTHEW 6: 1–8

'Don't show off in public. Your alms
Are between you and God! It just harms
Whatever you do
If it's not really true
To your calling. So watch the alarms!'

MATTHEW 6: 9–15

'Just pray to the Father. Give praise.
His Kingdom will come. Yes it stays!
Ask daily for bread
Forgive wrongs, and be led
To make up with each other! It pays!'

MATTHEW 6: 25–34

'Don't worry about what you'll wear
Or eat, 'cos you've nothing to fear.
The lilies don't wither,
The birds don't starve either!
And God provides everything here!'

MATTHEW 7: 15–21

'Beware of the people who dress
As wolves in sheep's clothing, no less!
Know folk by their fruits!
Bad roots bring bad shoots!
So make sure that your lives aren't a mess!'

MATTHEW 7: 24–27

'Make sure that you build upon rock
So your building will stand every knock!
If you build it on sand
Not a chance it will stand –
But collapse! And your neighbours will mock!'

MATTHEW 7: 28–29

Jesus taught with authority, not
As one of the scribes, who had got
His learning from books
Such were nothing but crooks –
And their teaching was all tommy rot!

MATTHEW 13: 24–30

A farmer who scattered some seeds
Saw them flourish, despite all the weeds.
But he gathered it all
Once the wheat had grown tall.
Sort the bad from the good, was his deed!

MATTHEW 13: 31

The tiniest seed in the store
Grew enormously larger, and more
Than the farmer expected
From seed he'd selected!
God's Kingdom is like that – be sure!

MATTHEW 13: 45–46

A merchant went looking for pearls
Entranced – just like men fall for girls.
Found the best one, so glad,
And sold all that he had,
Bought it up, like God's Kingdom unfurls.

MATTHEW 13: 47–48

The Kingdom of heaven's a net
That a fisherman casts out, to get
Enough fish to sell.
He kept some back as well,
Which he gave to his friends, and his pet.

MATTHEW 18: 23–35

A king reckoned up all the debt
That his servants incurred, and he bet
That if he forgave
Every one, it would pave
The example they also should set!

MATTHEW 20: 1–16

The manager went out to hire
Vineyard workers, in spite of the fire
Of the sun through the day,
When it came to their pay,
Their complaints taught them not to enquire!

MATTHEW 21: 28–31

Two sons were invited to work
For their father. One opted to shirk,
While the other said 'Yes.'
Both changed sides, to impress –
But the 'No' changed to 'Yes' won the perk!

MATTHEW 22: 2–14

'Please come to my feast,' said the king,
'The table is set, everything
Is ready for you!'
But the king really knew
That the guests more excuses would bring!

MATTHEW 24: 32–33

When the fig-tree displays its nice leaves,
You can tell, like the wheat stacked in sheaves,
That summer is near,
And the Kingdom is here,
When the Jesus disciple believes.

MATTHEW 25: 1–13

Ten girls to the wedding invited,
With oil in their lamps well ignited,
The groom came and passed,
But their oil did not last,
Only five of those girls got excited!

MATTHEW 25: 14–30

To servants, a man trusted funds,
Gave five, two and one, of his pounds.
'Please use them for good,
As you know that you should.
And don't bury your talents – like hounds!'

MARK 2: 21

'If you find that your coat has a tear,
And you've nothing else that you can wear,
Don't patch up the rent
With new cloth. You are meant
To know new and old just won't pair!'

MARK 2: 22

'If you use an old bottle for wine
That is old and mature, then that's fine.
But you really should know
That new wine should not go
Into old ones that don't glint and shine!'

MARK 4: 21

'If you have a lampstand with a light,
You know that it really is right
To light up the homestead
Not hide it below bed,
So nothing is hidden from sight!'

MARK 7: 15

'There's nothing that enters within
Which is anything near like a sin.
But all that comes out
Is like sin without doubt,
And defiles us all! True! Kith and kin!'

MARK 10: 13–16

When children were brought for His touch,
The disciples complained about such,
But Jesus defied them
With children beside Him,
He loved them, and cared for them much.

MARK 12: 1–12

'A man had a vineyard he prized,
Left his servants to tend it. Despised,
Those servants were killed
By the enemy. Willed
His revenge! All the enemy died!'

MARK 14: 43-49

'If you want to arrest me, why need
You come strongly armed? Yes, indeed
I was teaching each day
In the Temple. No way
Did you seize me!' But Scripture decreed.

MARK 14: 61-64

'You're the Christ are you?' asked the High Priest.
'The Son of The Blessed?' he teased.
'I am!' Jesus said.
High Priest raged crimson red.
'For blasphemy – death!' What a beast!

LUKE 1: 46-55

'My soul,' Mary said, 'full of joy!
My Saviour, my God – it's my boy!
His mercy's for nations
And all generations,
For ever. For Israel, Le Roi!'

LUKE 2: 4

From Nazareth Joseph departed
With Mary, and donkey that carted
Them both at a pace
To the Bethlehem place.
But baby, in stable, had started!

LUKE 2: 25–32

Simeon, righteous, devout
Received the Christ child without doubt.
'Now let me depart
Hence in peace!' From his heart –
'This Light here will never go out!'

LUKE 2: 41–42

We know nothing more of the lad
Till twelve years were passed, and he had
A Passover treat
To Jerusalem's seat
In the temple, with teachers. Not bad!

LUKE 2: 43–44

His parents were frantic with worry!
'No sign of the boy! We must hurry!'
Said Joseph to Mary
'It's really quite scary! –
Where can Jesus be?' Such a flurry!

LUKE 2: 46–49

Three days after, we're glad to relate
They found him engaged in debate
'It's my Father's business!'
Said Jesus. *'What is this?'*
Thought Mary, and pondered his fate.

LUKE 2: 51–52

Though neither could quite understand,
The three of them went hand in hand
Back to Nazareth town
Where the lad knuckled down
And became the best son in the land.

LUKE 4: 16–29

At Nazareth, as He would do
He read in the synagogue. True!
What He read from the books
Brought such terrible looks
From his hearers. They threw Him out! 'Shoo!'

LUKE 5: 10

'From henceforth, you're going to catch men!'
Said Jesus to Peter. 'What then –
Once fishing is done?'
'You'll catch men by the ton!'
He followed, but thought, 'Men? Like when?'

LUKE 9: 1–6

Disciples assembled, He said:
'Don't worry yourselves about bread.
You'll not need a thing!
Ditch your luggage! Just bring
Good News to all those where you're led!'

LUKE 9: 23–25

'To those who would follow me there,
Your cross, every day, you must bear!
For me, you may die
But your life is on high!
What you lose, you will gain! Is that clear?'

LUKE 9: 46–48

'Say, – who'll be the greatest? Please tell?
Your Kingdom sounds really quite swell!'
But Jesus looked round,
Saw a child on the ground.
'He's the greatest – this child!' Well, well, well!

LUKE 9: 50

'If you're really not for me, truly you know
It's fact – you're against me! Yes? No?'
This challenged them all,
But they heeded the call:
They were sure they were ready to go!

LUKE 10: 30–37

'From Jerusalem travelled a man
To Jericho. Sadly, he ran
Into bandits who mugged him,
Priests went by and shrugged him.
Sole helper – good Samaritan.'

LUKE 11: 5–10

'At midnight a friend rang the bell,
And begged for some bread. "What the hell?"
Said the sleeper, "You know
That it's midnight? E'en so,
A friend must be helped! Very well!"'

LUKE 11: 11–13

'What father, whose child begs for bread
Will offer him stones? Stones instead,
Or serpents for fish,
Or scorpions a dish,
Not the eggs that the child had expected?'

LUKE 12: 4–7

'Don't fear idle threats, in a word!
God loves you as the smallest bird!
You'll face threat and bluff,
And your lives may be tough!
That's the price you must pay! Yes – you heard!'

LUKE 12: 16–21

'A farmer's success was the tops,
But his barns were too small for the crops.
So he built more and bigger
Enhancing his vigour –
But losing his soul in the ops!'

LUKE 13: 6–9

'A vine didn't bear any fruit,
So the owner decided its root
Should be lifted at once.
But the gardener said, "Dunce!
Just manure it, and then watch it shoot!"'

LUKE 14:7-11

'At weddings, don't choose the best seat
Leave poshest ones for the elite.
Wear humility's gown,
It's the best in the town.
'Till the host says, "Come higher, and eat!"'

LUKE 15: 4-7

'A sheep strayed away from the flock,
Got lost in the wilderness rock.
The shepherd cared so.
Left the others. "Let's go
And retrieve it!" It's now under lock!'

LUKE 15: 8-10

'A woman's purse fell to the floor,
Coins missing, – just one, maybe more.
Getting down on her knee
She discovered it, see –
Gave the neighbours a party till four!'

LUKE 15: 11–32

'A son spent his father's bequest
On wine, women, song and the rest!
Too soon he went broke.
Eating pigs' food, he woke
To a joyful return, and a feast!'

LUKE 16: 1–13

'A steward owed pounds to his master.
Redeemed his lot very much faster
Being kind to his servants
Reducing their payments,
Commended as wise, not a waster!'

LUKE 16: 19–31

'A rich man had lived it up well.
After death, he descended to hell.
A poor man who died
Feasted on the far side –
A salutary warning to all!'

LUKE 18: 1–6

'A widow who pestered the judge
Couldn't get his attention to budge.
By keeping on at him
She finally got him
To take up her case! Wink, wink, nudge!'

LUKE 18: 9–14

'A Pharisee stood up to pray
With a flourish he knew what to say.
But a publican slowly
Knelt down, and bowed lowly,
And God hears his prayers to this day!'

LUKE 22: 42

Some time Jesus spent, deep in prayer,
The disciples he loved were all there.
'O Father, I pray
Take this cup far away!
Yet it's Your will, not mine, I declare!'

LUKE 22: 45–46

Gethsemane, near to the city,
Jerusalem's garden, so pretty.
Jesus asked them, *'Please stay*
Wide awake while I pray!'
But they fell fast asleep. Such a pity!

JOHN 1: 33

John baptised in Jordan's warm water.
When Jesus approached, did he oughta?
Voices speaking aloud
Were so plain to the crowd.
God's Spirit binds closer than mortar!

JOHN 2: 1–11

In Cana, a wedding was there.
The disciples and Jesus did share
The water made wine –
Quite miraculously fine,
And the wedding remarkably rare!

JOHN 4: 5–26

A woman Samaritan met
At a well, Jesus resting, 'You'll get
Living water from me,'
Jesus said. *'Just you see!*
It is I who am speaking! I'm He!'

JOHN 4: 24–26

God is Holy Spirit, you see,
We worship Him, both One and Three.
Jesus enters the world
With His Kingdom unfurled,
And to everyone says, 'I am He!'

JOHN 5: 1–9

In a pool called Bethesda, they say,
Many sick people came day by day.
A cripple in tears,
After thirty long years,
Was restored to good health – Jesus' way!

JOHN 6: 1

The crowds followed Jesus all day,
They had come with him most of the way.
In a boat, off the coast
A few metres at most,
He taught them what Christians should say!

JOHN 6: 1–14

A crowd had been round Him for hours
'They'll be hungry,' said Jesus. His powers
To feed them He used
With compassion, He mused –
'Fish and bread, more than ever, are yours!'

JOHN 6: 16–21

It was evening as they crossed the sea
When a storm whipped the waves to frenzy.
'Help, Master, we sink!'
They were right on the brink
Of drowning. Said Jesus: *'Calm be!'*

JOHN 6: 52–59

In the synagogue, Jesus decreed,
'*My life is the life you should lead!*
Food and drink in my Name
It's my Spirit — the same!
I'm alive in you, each time you feed!'

JOHN 8: 51–59

Abraham's nation, Hebrews
Always sought the Messiah. The Jews
In centuries later
Met Jesus, Creator,
Pre-Abraham — yet today's News!

JOHN 9: 1–12

There was a man blind from his birth:
A wretched existence on earth.
But Jesus came by
And anointed his eye.
Now his sight makes his life doubly worth!

JOHN 10: 1–5

If you want to steal sheep from the fold
You'll have to make sure you are bold,
For the shepherd who's true
Watches out, just for you!
So beware – sheep know strangers, of old!

JOHN 11: 1–44

In Bethany Lazarus died,
Mary, Martha, his sisters – they cried.
But Jesus gave orders
'Depart the tomb's borders!'
And Lazarus lively complied!

JOHN 12: 1–8

At a meal in a Bethany home,
Relaxing with Jesus, did come
Mary Magdalene, sweet
Ointment bathing his feet.
Judas groaned, 'You're a wastrel, sell some!'

JOHN 12: 12–16

It was Passover time very soon,
And we know it was nearly full moon.
  '*A donkey for Master*
  Will get Him there faster!'
Jerusalem bound, before noon.

JOHN 13: 1–11

The Passover meal had begun
When Jesus approached Number One:
  '*I'll now wash your feet!*'
  Peter jumped from his seat –
'*Wash my feet, wash the lot! All in one!*'

JOHN 13: 21–30

During supper, the Passover meal,
Jesus sensed his disciples' appeal.
  '*There'll be one of you here*
  Who'll betray me, I fear!'
'*Is it I Lord? Oh please do reveal!*'

JOHN 13: 30

It was Judas who dipped in the bowl
At the same time as Jesus. His soul
Was bedevilled by Satan.
Remorse quickly set in.
'*Betray Him!*' – the Sanhedrin's goal.

JOHN 13: 34–35

'*A commandment I give to you now,*'
Said Jesus, '*A new one, shows how*
You should love one another,
And not hurt each other.
That way, my disciples will grow!'

JOHN 14: 1–6

'*You must never be worried by fear*'
Jesus said, '*Never fear, with me near!*
I'll prepare you a place
In my house. And my face
Will always precede you from here!'

JOHN 14: 16

'Just listen, and learn it from me,
I tell you the truth, don't you see –
Once the Comforter's come,
You'll just witness and roam
With the power and the love of JC!'

JOHN 14: 18

'If you love me, you'll do what I say,'
Said Jesus, 'and I'll point the way.
I'll never forsake you
Nor leave you, but take you
With me on the heavenly way.'

JOHN 14: 25–31

'For yourselves, you will soon have to fend'
Said Jesus, 'But it's not the end.
Your love and your power
Will increase hour by hour,
And the world will eventually bend!'

JOHN 15: 1-11

'If you've ever seen grapes on the vine,
Your life is entwined, yours with mine,
When your roots are all healthy,
And harvesting wealthy,
The spiritual fruit is the wine!'

JOHN 16: 13

'When the Spirit is come, he will guide you
To truth, that will soon be inside you.
You'll know what to say
When you're asked on the day!
You will go with my presence beside you!'

JOHN 16: 28-31

The disciples all said, 'It's now plain,
We never need ask you again!
You came forth from God,
We believe you're The Lord,
And it's our job the whole world to gain!'

JOHN 18: 12–14

Jesus first went to Annas for trial,
Then Caiaphas, equally vile.
With Passover nigh
One man still had to die.
With or without Peter's denial!

JOHN 18: 27

Simon Peter was there at the court
Of the High Priest. A maid quickly thought
'Jesus' fellow, I'm sure!'
Peter cursed and he swore.
The cock crowed third time, and he wept.

JOHN 19: 15

They took Jesus out to the cross.
'King of Jews' was his title. No loss
Felt by Pontius Pilate.
Rage turned red to violet –
The Jews screamed, 'He's never our boss!'

JOHN 19: 16

Pilate asked Jesus: 'King of the Jews?'
'As you say,' answered Jesus. 'Bad news'
Thought Pilate, 'I dare not
Have rivals. I care not –
Let one prisoner die. Jews, you choose!'

JOHN 19: 20–22

In Latin, and Hebrew, and Greek,
Was the title of Jesus. A peek
When they took at the cross
Jews saw Pilate was boss!
'What is written is written! I speak!'

JOHN 19: 23–25

For His garments the soldiers cast lots,
His coat alone must have cost pots!
Then they raised Him aloft
On the cross, nails in soft
Flesh. The victim of dastardly plots!

JOHN 19: 25–30

Jesus said very little that hour.
Words could scarcely display divine power.
To His mother, *'Take John'*
He said, *'Now take your son.'*
As He died, so His life did outpour.

JOHN 19: 33

The soldiers had had a long day.
'Dispose of the criminals, yea!
We'll break their legs so
To make sure that they go!'
But Jesus was dead. 'All OK!'

JOHN 19: 38

From Arimathea, so sad,
A councillor, Joseph, who had
A rock tomb nearby
Where Jesus could lie.
Pilate gave him the body. So glad.

JOHN 19: 39–42

They bound Jesus' body with spice
And buried Him there in a trice.
With Passover near,
They'd a race to get clear.
Set a guard on the tomb. Cold as ice.

JOHN 20: 1–3

Mary ran to the locked Upper Room.
All her knocking was useless. Boom! Boom!
'*I've just seen the Lord!*
He is Risen, adored!'
'*Let's go see!*' Peter, John – off they zoom!

JOHN 20: 4–9

Peter reached the tomb well after John.
It was true. Jesus' body had gone!
Empty tomb. Body nil!
Yet the grave-clothes were still
As they'd left them. Could this be a con?

JOHN 20: 16

Mary went to that tomb Sunday morning.
The stone was removed, without warning.
She stood back in tears,
'*Come on, Mary!*' she hears,
'*Your Lord is arisen! No mourning!*'

JOHN 20: 19–21

The Upper Room, Monday that week,
When the doors were still locked. Not a squeak
As He strode 'cross the floor
'*I'll be with you some more!*
Peace be with you!' he said. Fantastique!

JOHN 20: 24–29

It was Thomas who missed Jesus. '*Shame! -
I must see for myself!*' was his claim.
'*So reach out and touch*'
Jesus said, '*wounds and such.*'
'*My Lord and my God! That's Your Name!*'

JOHN 21: 1

Days later, his friends went out fishing,
And secretly, each of them wishing
That Jesus was risen.
When just past the mizzen,
He stood! 'Be at peace!' was his greeting.

JOHN 21: 1–14

'Been working all night, with no sight
Of a fish?' Jesus said, 'To the right –
Just cast your nets out!'
One-five-three fish about
Landed up in the hold. What a bite!

JOHN 21: 15–18

A barbecue later that morning
Set Peter's true loyalty dawning.
Asked Jesus, 'You love me?'
'Of course!' 'Reassure me! –
Feed sheep, lambs, and sheep! Just a warning!'

JOHN 21: 25

There are so many things Jesus said,
And did – words that you have just read.
'If we wrote every one
We'd need books by the ton!
We could never complete it!' John said.

ACTS 2: 4

Filled full of sadness and gloom
When the Spirit roared into the room.
On fire for their Lord,
They all shouted His Word
In Jerusalem, Rome and Khartoum!

ACTS 2: 42

They heard the apostles' strong teaching,
They prayed, and they spent the time preaching.
They found that the Word
Which they spread, people heard
In their hundreds! The message was reaching!

ACTS 3:1–10

When Peter and John were at prayer
They saw a man beckon and stare.
'Have you got a few bob?'
Healed him! Right proper job!
'In the name of Lord Jesus, we care!'

ACTS 5: 34–42

Gamaliel, Pharisee there,
Wisely urged, *'The apostles we spare!'*
'If this is of God,
It will pass on the nod!
But if not, it will vanish! Thin air!'

ACTS 6: 1–7

The Grecian widows out there
Said mealtimes were simply not fair.
'We're being neglected!'
And so they elected
Seven deacons, to give them fair share!

ACTS 7: 54–55

Now Stephen upset all the Jews
By fearlessly preaching Good News.
They stoned him to death.
As he took his last breath –
Saw a vision of heaven! Such views!

ACTS 8: 1–3

It was Saul who had seen Stephen's death,
Convinced it was God's will on earth:
That all Christians should die.
He determined, 'Yes I
Will eliminate Christians at birth!'

ACTS 8: 14–17

They laid hands on all of the band
And prayed that God's Spirit would land
On all who were true,
So that everyone knew
The Lord Jesus, our God, was on hand.

ACTS 8: 26–40

Towards Ethiopia fast
A eunuch in chariot passed
Our Philip, who duly
Gave baptism truly.
'Behold, here is water!' At last!

ACTS 9: 1–18

Saul, breathing threatening and slaughter,
Killed dad and mum – yes – son and daughter.
On Damascus' road,
Jesus called him, aloud!
He became Paul, the Christian's aorta!

ACTS 9: 17–19

Ananias was bolder than most,
For Saul he became Christian host.
He laid hands on Saul,
Baptised him as Paul,
And helped him receive Holy Ghost.

ACTS 10: 9–13

In Joppa, the sunshine drenched Peter,
Who dreamed God had plans for him neater.
'*Let all Gentile Jews*
Ignore Jewish views' –
Now Peter of meat he's an eater!

ACTS 18: 1–6

When first the Good News went abroad,
Only Jews thought that they knew the Lord.
Each day it was clear
As the Gentiles got near
They were Christians as well, 'pon my Word.

ACTS 20: 7–12

It was Eutychus, young lad, well-spoken
Who fell asleep, rudely awoken
While Paul preached for hours,
He fell into the flowers
From the window above. Nothing broken!

ACTS 28: 1–7

A storm arose while Paul was sailing
His tummy was bilious and ailing.
He prayed more than most,
Got shipwrecked on the coast –
Northeast Malta, with friendship prevailing.

ACTS 28: 30–31

Eventually Paul got to Rome,
Spending two years there, in his home.
He worked making tents
Preaching Christ to the gents,
Until finally, God called him: 'Come!'

A note about Romans

Paul wrote Romans in AD 57. Romans 13:14
Converted Augustine in 387. Romans 1:17
Converted Luther in 1517, and Luther's preface
to Romans converted Wesley in 1738.

The letter to Romans, of Paul,
The man who was once known as Saul,
Converted Augustine,
And Luther, and just in
Was Wesley – remarkable haul!

ROMANS 1: 16–17

The gospel has fantastic power.
It enters the soul hour by hour.
The Jews first, then Greeks
Hear the words Spirit speaks,
With the strength of a spiritual tower!

ROMANS 6: 4

We were buried with Christ in the tomb
Yet His new life broke out of that womb.
If we're dead unto sin
It's His life that we're in,
That disperses the old gloom and doom!

ROMANS 8: 22

At present, the world groans in pain,
Till Jesus the Christ comes again!
We wait our redemption
And eagerly mention
The spiritual prize we will gain!

ROMANS 8: 35

There's nothing can force us apart
With the love of Christ deep in our heart!
Not trouble, or hurry,
Or famine, or worry,
Or peril, or sword, or sin's dart!

ROMANS 8: 38–39

There's nothing God's love cannot beat,
Whether life, death, in depths, or in height.
Nor angels, nor powers,
Principalities. Ours
Are lives in His hands, till we meet!

ROMANS 12: 4–5

Although we are many, yet we
Are the Body of Jesus, you see!
His ears, eyes, and mouth,
East and west, north and south,
We are one on this earth! So is He!

ROMANS 13: 13–14

Walk honestly, as in the day.
Let each behave decently, yea!
Don't drunkenly revel
Or live like the Devil,
But always proclaim Jesus' way!

ROMANS 14 – 16

So, whether we live or we die,
Please God by example and try
To live as we should
For we know that it's good
In God's sight! And that's all folks – Bye bye!

1 CORINTHIANS 11: 23–25

Betrayed, Jesus spoke up, and He
Broke bread, and He gave it. 'You'll *see* –
My body is this –
And my blood.' (It was His!)
'Just do this in memory of me!'

1 CORINTHIANS 12: 4–11

Want spiritual gifts to be thine?
Maybe wisdom, or knowledge? That's fine!
Or miracle working
Or prophetic talking,
Discernment, or tongues? It's divine!

1 CORINTHIANS 12: 12–31

The Church is a body of sorts,
With head, hands, heart, feet, even warts!
All parts need to function
Within Spirit's unction,
And share joy or sadness, and thoughts.

1 CORINTHIANS 13

If I speak without love, then I am
Just hollow, my life is a sham!
As a child, I was child-like
But now, I am Christ-like,
With faith, hope, love! Yes, Sir! Yes, Ma'am!

1 CORINTHIANS 14: 19

In Church, yes, it's better by far:
To speak five words, that so clearly are
Understood by us all –
Where ten thousand appal –
Verbal gobbledygook is a bar!

1 CORINTHIANS 14: 40

If you're going to do anything well,
You should heed what St Paul has to tell:
'Let all things you do
Be done decently too,
And in order.' Does that ring a bell?

1 CORINTHIANS 15: 12–19

If Christ never rose from the dead,
It shouldn't have even been *said*!
But the empty tomb's shock
Gave the Jews a real knock –
Made their guards' faces blush rather red!

2 CORINTHIANS 3: 6

Good laws deserve to be made.
We agree that they should be obeyed.
But the Spirit gives life
Where the law just brings strife,
The more so when it's been man-made!

2 CORINTHIANS 9: 7

If you're giving God some of your money
For the work of His Church, it's not funny
To grudgingly spare
What you grudgingly share.
Give cheerfully! Be bright and sunny!

2 CORINTHIANS 13: 14

The grace of Christ Jesus our Lord,
The love of God – all this is stored –
The fellowship too
Of His Spirit, with you!
Three in One! God forever adored!

GALATIANS 3: 28

You might be a Greek, or a Jew,
Or female or male, but it's true
Whether servant or free
We are *one* – don't you see –
One in Christ! That means us! I and you!

GALATIANS 5: 22–23

The fruit of the Spirit's for you:
Love, joy, peace – are Spirit-fruit too!
Longsuffering, kindness,
Goodness and faithfulness,
Meekness and temperance. True!

EPHESIANS 4: 15

If we fight, or we argue, or moan,
And criticise harshly, or groan,
There is one thing to know:
Wherever we go
Speak in love! It's our spiritual phone!

EPHESIANS 6: 10–18

Put on the whole armour of God.
Our fight is against flesh and blood.
It means we will stand
In the evil day, and
Defeat evil powers as we should!

EPHESIANS 6: 10–18

Stand, therefore, with truth round your frame
And righteousness' breastplate, the same.
Your feet shod with peace
Deflect darts, as if grease,
And the helmet and sword? Spirit's flame!

PHILIPPIANS 2: 5–10

Be careful to see that your mind
Is the same as in Jesus you find.
He served us, so humble.
The Cross makes us stumble.
Accept God's instructions, defined!

PHILIPPIANS 4: 7

The peace that I give you, of God
Passes all understanding. A rod
And a staff there to guide you,
A haven to hide you.
Christ's way, hearts and minds will have trod.

PHILIPPIANS 4: 11–12

I try to be fairly content.
Things go wrong – even things that are meant
To go right, but they don't.
It's a test when they won't.
But with Jesus, it's all heaven-sent!

COLOSSIANS 1: 9

We pray for you all, every day,
And want you to know why we say:
'Fill up to the brim
With the knowledge of Him!' –
And be wise in the spiritual way!

COLOSSIANS 3: 16

When Jesus speaks deep in your thought,
You'll teach and behave as you ought,
Singing psalms all day long
Hymns and spiritual song –
This is *God's grace!* It cannot be bought!

COLOSSIANS 3: 18–23

Be gentle and kind in your life,
It's better to love! There's no strife
Where family and friends
Really *do* make amends –
That's children, and husband, and wife!

COLOSSIANS 3: 23–24

Whatever you think, say, or do,
Just do it for Jesus! And you
Will get your reward –
Not from men – but the Lord!
And you know this is right! Yes – it's true!

1 THESSALONIANS 4: 14–18

We long to be one with the Lord,
For this is His promise, His word:
At the trumpet blast sound,
When the voice shouts around –
We're caught up in the air – *'Come aboard!'*

1 THESSALONIANS 5: 1–6

We don't know the time or the place
When we meet Jesus Christ face to face,
But we have to be ready
And sober and steady,
And watchful. On guard – just in case!

1 THESSALONIANS 5: 12–18

Encouragement! This is the clue
To build up the fellowship. True!
Look after the weak,
And keep order, and speak
Peace, and joy! Always pray – God loves *you*!

2 THESSALONIANS 1: 3–12

When things go so terribly wrong,
And it's hard for you to get along,
Just trust in the Lord
And take Him at His word!
'*The Lord is our Saviour!*' – our song!

1 TIMOTHY 5: 18

Let an ox without muzzle grind corn.
Pay workers their dues night and morn.
To do the Lord's work
Is the worthiest perk,
If it's teaching to which you are born!

1 TIMOTHY 5: 23

Timothy, Bishop much later
Of Ephesus, drank no more water.
'Drink wine for the sake
Of your tummy, and make
Your life purer!' was what Paul had taught. Ah!

2 TIMOTHY 1: 13–14

I pray that the gift which God gave you
Develops and grows. Let it save you!
Your faith will grow strong
As you journey along!
But hold fast to my teachings, I pray you!

2 TIMOTHY 4: 7–8

I fought the good fight to the end!
I finished the course. I'll not bend
From the doctrine of Christ.
I'll back Him to the last!
And a rightousness crown He will send!

2 TIMOTHY 4: 11–13

Dear Luke is the only one with me.
Take Mark, and bring him, as well, with thee.
Find the parchment and books
And my cloak on the hooks
Left with Carpus, at Troas – my dear T!

TITUS 1: 7

It's very important to know
How a Christian person should go:
No brawling or striking
And don't get a liking
For lucre so filthy! No, no!

TITUS 1: 8

A bishop should set an example
And really be Christlike. A sample:
Be sober, and you should
Be temperate and good
And faithful. Encourage your people!

PHILEMON

A slave who has left you in haste?
Invite him to come back. Don't waste
The chance to make up,
Without punishment. Sup
Together as friends now! Act fast!

HEBREWS 1

Whoever wrote Hebrews, he wrote
Encouraging Christians to note
That things will get better!
Please search through this letter!
'*Best literary Greek!*' – so they quote!

HEBREWS 2

It speaks of Christ Jesus the man
Above all the angels. How can
We fail to adore Him
And trust Him? Our anthem
In rough times – He'll not let us down!

HEBREWS 10: 4

To take away sins, it was thought
That animal sacrifice sought
Forgiveness divine
Of the wrongs – yours and mine.
But atonement can never be bought!

HEBREWS 10: 25

It's easy to think we don't need
To meet up together. But we'd
Do better to meet
Far more often, and greet
And encourage each other! Indeed!

HEBREWS 11

By faith, men of old lived their lives.
By faith, so we read, did their wives.
The lesson we learn
Is so plain. We discern
That their faith was as sharp as sharp knives!

HEBREWS 13: 5

Don't get an obsession for money
Like bees that are dazzled by honey,
Remember the teaching
Of Jesus, His preaching:
'*You can't take it with you!*' That's funny!

HEBREWS 13: 8

There's one thing that time will not sever:
Our Jesus – the same, now and ever.
He'll always be here,
And He'll bring us good cheer!
And He'll never forsake us! That's *never*!

HEBREWS 13: 20

The Shepherd of all faithful sheep
Our God of all peace – He will keep
Our hearts and our minds
In perfection. He binds
Us all in one flock. A clean sweep!

JAMES 2: 20–24

It's something we've all got to do –
Be doers, not just hearers, who
Hear all that is said
But delude ourselves! Dead
Religion is vain! Yes – it's true!

JAMES 5: 14

Is any among you not well?
It's better for us if you tell
The Church who will pray
With you all, day by day.
Anointing and healing. That's swell!

1 Peter 2: 1

Put wickedness into the bin!
Hypocrisy, guile – they're all sin!
To envy is wrong,
Or speak evil. Be strong!
And *that* way, the Devil won't win!

1 Peter 2: 7

The stone which the builders rejected,
The cornerstone safely erected!
It's Jesus we mean
And it's plain to be seen
That in Jesus our life is perfected!

1 Peter 3: 8

Like-minded, compassionate – you
Must be tenderhearted, you too!
In humbleness live,
And for evil don't give
Evil back! That's your blessing! It's true!

1 PETER 5: 8

Be sober, be vigilant, while
Your enemy – devillish guile,
With a lion's great roar
Devours all the poor
In his way! Whom resist every mile!

1 PETER 5: 10

It's God who has called you in grace.
In suffering, Christ takes first place
He's first in your life.
He'll perfect you in strife
As he strengthens you all, face to face.

2 PETER

Possibly it's the last letter
Written in the NT. Better
To see it construed
As a re-write of Jude,
Used by 2 Peter as a trendsetter!

1 JOHN 2: 1–2

If any man sin, we have found
In Jesus, an Advocate sound.
He mediates now
Though we need not ask how –
As we know we're forgiven all round!

1 JOHN 3: 2

Children of God now are we,
Though we don't know in what way. We'll see
Our Lord as He is
And be like Him – be His!
That's the promise for us, from JC!

1 JOHN 3: 18

To love someone, love has to be
Something done, not just said, don't you see!
In deed and in truth
In old age and in youth –
He commands us all in 1 John 3.

1 JOHN 4: 18

Perfect love casts out all fear!
It's true, and we know year by year
That whoever receives this
Will always believe this!
Love God, for He's always so near!

2 JOHN

The second Epistle of John
In thirteen short verses – it's gone!
But the message we get
Is of love – love and yet
It needs to be said – on and on!

3 JOHN

3 John is as short. One verse more
Than 2 John, and yet he still saw
That Christians do better
Despite his short letter
Providing they value verse 4!

JUDE

This letter, to Christians all over
The world – though at first Asia Minor –
Encourages all
To rise up, when we fall,
And shelter beneath Spirit's cover!

REVELATION 1: 8–9

'True: Alpha and Omega, I'm
The first and the last, and the same.
I promise to be
Here for you, don't you see –
For I was, and will be, and I AM.'

REVELATION 1: 11

To Asian Churches wrote John,
Ephesus, Smyrna, Perg'mum,
Thyatira and Sardis,
Philadelphia – oh yes –
And Laodicaea! All done!

REVELATION 3: 14–16

In Laodicaea, the form
Of the Christians was only lukewarm!
'Be one or the other
My dear Christian brother!
Not cold, warm, but hot! That's the norm!'

REVELATION 4

The vision of heaven was one
Surrounded by jewels. A throne,
Twenty elders, and creatures
With fantastic features –
Prostrated, in worship begun.

REVELATION 4 – 6

In secret, the Christians met there.
Symbolic, the language, they share.
Such as, 'Lamb', ' scrolls', and 'seals',
'Angels', 'creatures', and 'wheels':
All revealed – to the reader aware!

REVELATION 7: 1–4

The servants of God bore a mark
On their foreheads, the spiritual spark
Which set them apart
Setting fire to the heart
Lighting 144 three-os in dark.

REVELATION 11: 15–19

The angel's sound – yes, number seven
Was followed by voices in heaven.
Then worship took place
Amidst thunder apace,
And opened God's temple for all men.

REVELATION 13

The Emperor, Roman Domitian
Was puzzled by number addition.
His dastardly tricks
Totalled six-sixty-six.
He was Antichrist, Beast. Evil mission!